CHILDREN'S REFERENCE
THE HUMAN BODY

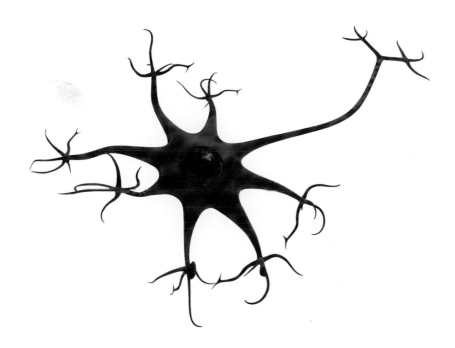

Capella

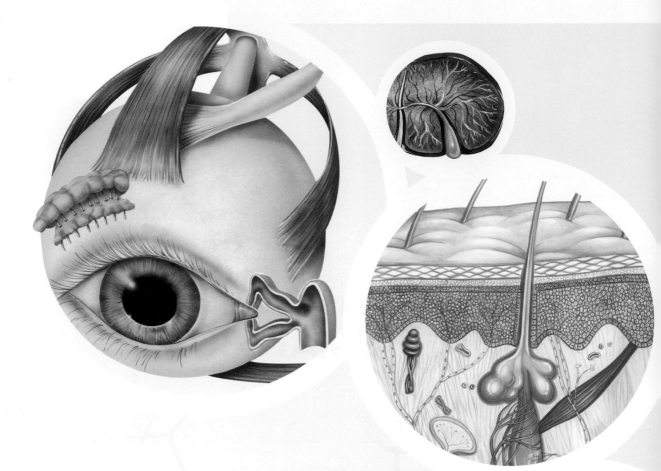

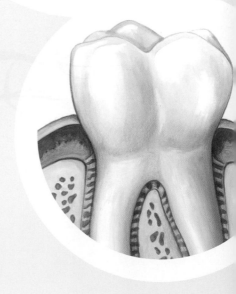

This edition published in 2008 by Arcturus Publishing Limited
26/27 Bickels Yard, 151–153 Bermondsey Street,
London SE1 3HA

Copyright © 2008 Arcturus Publishing Limited

All rights reserved. No part of this publication may be reproduced,
stored in a retrieval system, or transmitted, in any form or by any
means, electronic, mechanical, photocopying, recording or otherwise,
without written permission in accordance with the provisions of the
Copyright Act 1956 (as amended). Any person or persons who do
any unauthorised act in relation to this publication may be liable to
criminal prosecution and civil claims for damages.

ISBN: 978-1-84193-821-9

Designers: Q2A India and Talking Design
Editors: Rebecca Gerlings and Alex Woolf

Printed in China

Contents

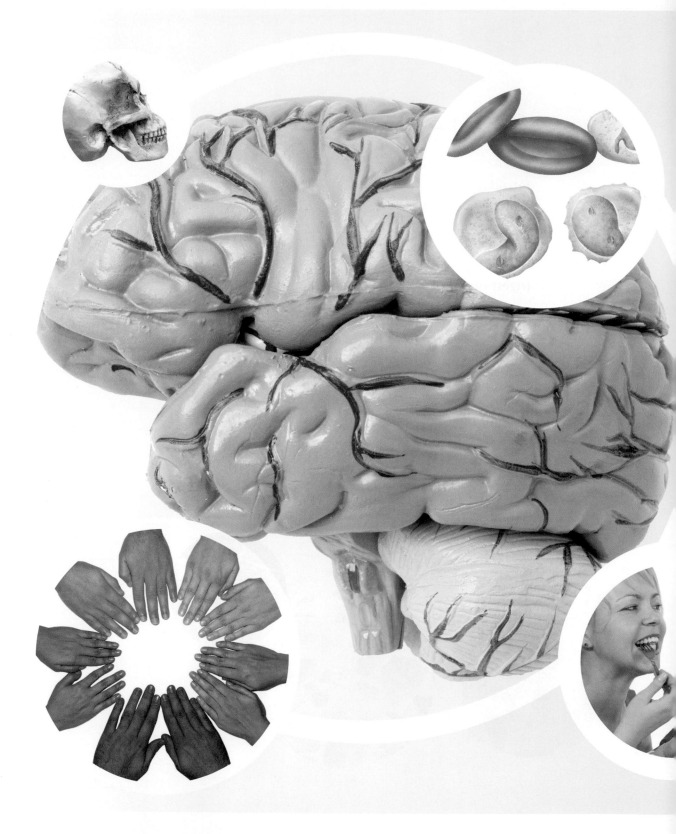

Introduction

The human body is something that is easily take for granted. But if we look at how it works, we start to understand how extraordinary and complex it really is. Whenever we enjoy a meal, ride a bike, or have a conversation with a friend, complex processes are taking place inside our body that enable us to do these things. Each part of our body has its own special job, and it is often only when a part goes wrong—through illness or disease, for example—that we start to appreciate how important it is.

In this book, you will discover many fascinating facts about the human body. For example, how do we transform food into energy? How do our ears hear? What does the inside of a muscle look like? How do we fight germs? You can find out the answers to these questions and many more in the pages of this book.

External Body Parts

The population of the world is more than six and a half billion, yet no two people can look completely alike. There are always differences in the color and elasticity of our skin, the shape of our muscles, the amount of fat within our bodies, and the size and shape of our skeletons. However, all human beings have the same body parts. The visible parts of the human body include the skin, hair, nails, hands, and feet.

Key facts:

• The body continuously sheds tiny particles of dead skin. It grows completely new skin at least once every month. It is estimated that a human being sheds at least 18 kilograms (40 pounds) of skin in their lifetime.

• The kind of hair a person has is determined by the shape of their hair follicles. Asians have round follicles, Europeans have round to oval, and Africans have flat follicles. Straight hair grows out of round follicles and curly or frizzy hair out of flat follicles.

• The palms and fingers of human hands have ridged patterns. This ridged texture helps us to grasp and hold things better. These patterns are unique—no two people can have identical ones.

▶ **Getting under the skin**
A cross-section of the skin showing various layers.

Skin is the largest organ of the human body. It is a protective covering that prevents too much heat or harmful bacteria from entering the body. It also prevents the body from losing too much water and other nutrients. Skin is made up of three layers—the epidermis, the dermis, and fat. The epidermis is the outermost layer and is made up of a thin layer of dead cells that are replaced continuously. When the dead cells wear away, new cells are formed. A substance called keratin makes the epidermis tough and waterproof.

The epidermis also produces melanin, a substance that protects the skin from the harmful rays of the sun. The dermis is a thicker and more elastic layer. It contains follicles from which hair grows. It also contains sebaceous glands, which produce an oily substance called sebum that keeps the skin from becoming dry and cracked. Sweat glands secrete water and salt from the body and are situated in the dermis. This layer also has sensory nerves, which help the skin to feel sensations and changes in temperature. The fat layer is responsible for storing energy and keeping the body warm.

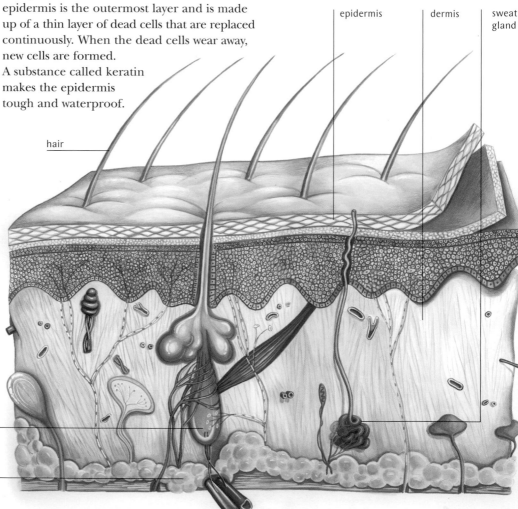

epidermis | dermis | sweat gland

hair

hair root

fat layer

Hair and nails

Hair grows out of the skin all over the body, except on the lips, the soles of the feet, and the palms of the hands. Hair is made of keratin, the same substance that is found in the outermost layer of skin. The nails on fingers and toes are attached by their roots, which fit into grooves in the skin. Nails are flexible and hornlike in appearance. The roots of nails produce new cells, which make the nail grow. This means that the oldest part of the nail is at the fingertip.

◄ Flexible fingers
Fingers are flexible because each of them is made up of three separate bones called phalanges, while thumbs have two phalanges each.

◄ Hardy nails
Nails protect the soft skin of our fingers from injuries and bacteria. We are able to cut our nails without feeling any pain because they do not have nerves. This is also the case with our hair.

Limbs

Human beings use their hands and feet for various activities. They are two of the most useful parts of the human body. A hand consists of a palm, a wrist, and five fingers, or digits, including the thumb. The wrist is a flexible bone that attaches the hand to the forearm. Our two hands are mirror images of each other. Fingertips have sensory nerves, which help us to feel texture, temperature, and pain. Feet are essential for movement and balance. The human foot is made up of six parts—ankle, heel, instep, sole, ball, and toes. The ankle connects the foot to the leg, while the toes help in gripping and walking. The ball is the soft spongy part located just behind the toes. The heel and the arch (the curve found at the bottom of the foot) support the body and absorb shock while walking or running. The instep is the raised, curved part on top of the foot, between the ankle and the toes.

ankle

heel

instep

sole

ball

▲ Best foot forward
Humans use their legs and feet for a variety of activities like walking, running, and dancing. Most of the body weight is carried by the two largest bones in the feet.

Natural protection

The skin color of different races is determined by a substance called melanin, which is present in the epidermis. There are two types of melanin—pheomelanin, which ranges from red to yellow in color, and eumelanin, which is dark brown to black. Light-skinned people have pheomelanin, and that is why they get sunburned easily. Dark skinned people, on the other hand, have eumelanin, which protects them against the ultraviolet rays of the Sun.

> ## Try these too:
>
> Bones and Joints (p 10–11), The Heart and Circulation (p 18–19), The Brain and Nervous System (p 24–25), Falling Sick (p 28–29)

Bones and Joints

The skeleton is a framework of bones, which gives shape to the human body. The skeleton of an adult human being consists of 206 bones. These bones not only protect the internal organs of the human body, but also support the muscles connected to it.

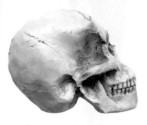

▲ **Heady issues**
The skull consists of the cranium and facial bones. The cranium is a bony case that protects the brain.

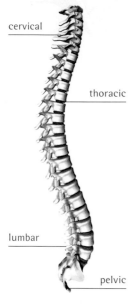

cervical

thoracic

lumbar

pelvic

▲ **Spinal curves**
When seen from the side, the backbone is curved at four different regions. These regions are called cervical (neck), thoracic (upper trunk), lumbar (lower back), and pelvic. The curves allow for an increased flexibility and provide more room for the internal organs.

The bones that make up the skeleton are hard on the outside and spongy on the inside. This reduces their weight. Deep inside the larger bones is bone marrow, which produces blood cells. Bones also store calcium and phosphate, two important body-building minerals. The skeleton consists of the skull, the backbone, the ribcage, the shoulder and hip girdles, and the bones of the arms and legs. Arm bones are attached to the body at the shoulder blade and leg bones are attached to the hipbone, or pelvis.

Facial bones
The skull is a hard shell made up of 28 bones fused together. It gives shape to the face and protects the brain. The only skull bone that is not completely fixed is the jawbone. The jawbone is hinged below the ear, so it can move up and down easily.

The spine
The spine, or backbone, supports the body and protects the delicate spinal cord. It is made up of 33 vertebrae that are joined together. The last bone is longer than the rest of the vertebrae. It is triangular in shape and looks like a tail. The ribcage is connected to the backbone at the back and to the breastbone at the front. It forms a protective cover for the heart and lungs.

Soft bones
Some parts of our body are shaped by cartilage instead of bone. Cartilage is more flexible than bone, but it is also damaged or worn out more easily. The nose, ear, ribs, and throat are made of cartilage. Small discs of cartilage are also present between each of the vertebrae in the backbone.

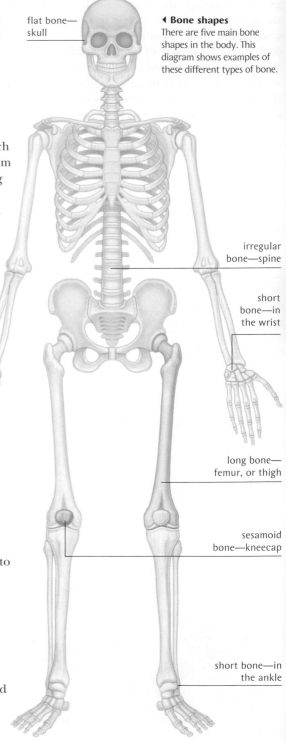

flat bone—skull

◀ **Bone shapes**
There are five main bone shapes in the body. This diagram shows examples of these different types of bone.

irregular bone—spine

short bone—in the wrist

long bone—femur, or thigh

sesamoid bone—kneecap

short bone—in the ankle

Inside bones

Most bones have a tough outer layer that contains nerves and blood vessels. Inside this is a strong, hard layer made of a material called compact bone. Blood vessels and nerves run through holes in the compact bone to the inner layer, called spongy bone. Spongy bone is a mesh of bone pieces. A soft jelly called bone marrow fills the spaces between them. Red bone marrow, found at the ends of bones, helps to produce red blood cells. Yellow bone marrow, found in the middle areas of bones, is mainly fat. Bones are living tissues, just like the rest of the body. The blood vessels running through the bones bring oxygen and nutrients for the bones to use. They also carry away waste chemicals that the bones produce. Bones need to communicate with the brain. The nerves in the bones carry information to the brain about bone pain or damage.

▾ Not so solid
The outside of a bone is hard, and the bone itself looks solid. But they are made up of several different layers, complete with a blood supply and nerves.

tough outer layer

bone marrow

spongy bone

compact bone

blood vessel

Key facts:

• Human beings are born with about 300 bones. The bones of new born babies are soft and flexible. As they grow, some of these bones fuse, or join together, and the skeleton becomes strong and tough.

• The hyoid bone is a small U-shaped bone in the neck that supports the tongue. It is the only floating bone in the body. This means that the hyoid is not attached to any other bone in the body. Instead, the hyoid bone is well supported by the muscles in the neck.

• Most joints are covered by a ligament layer called a capsule. Inside this is a thin layer called a synovial membrane. This makes a special fluid that helps to lubricate the joint, so that the bones can move easily past each other.

Try these too:

External Body Parts (p 8–9), Muscles (p 12–13), Digestion and Excretion (p 14–15), The Heart and Circulation (p 18–19), Falling Sick (p 28–29)

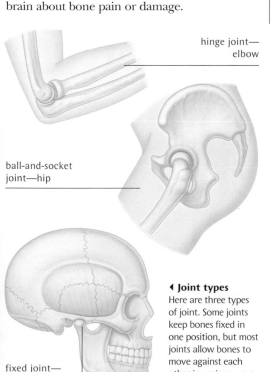

hinge joint—elbow

ball-and-socket joint—hip

fixed joint—skull

◄ Joint types
Here are three types of joint. Some joints keep bones fixed in one position, but most joints allow bones to move against each other in various ways.

Mineral store

Nearly three quarters of bone material is made up of minerals such as calcium, phosphorus, magnesium, and zinc. Bones act as a mineral store for the body. If the body has plenty of calcium, the bones will store any that is not needed. If there is too little calcium, the bones will release some for use by other parts of the body.

Joints

Bones are stiff and cannot bend. We can bend our arms and legs because bones meet at joints, which are flexible. The main types of moveable joints in the human body include pivot, hinge, and ball-and-socket joints. Pivot joints allow the bone to rotate and move up and down. Hinge joints allow the bone to move up and down, or backward and forward. Ball-and-socket joints are the most flexible and allow the bone to move in many different ways. The fixed joints do not move at all—the skull bones, for example.

Muscles

Between the skin and the skeleton are the muscles that help the body to move. There are three types of muscles—skeletal, smooth, and heart muscles.

Skeletal muscles are attached to the bones. They are called voluntary muscles because they can be easily controlled. Smooth muscle forms part of the walls of the digestive organs, such as the stomach, intestines, and the kidneys, helping food move along the digestive system. The heart muscle, also known as the cardiac muscle, is a very strong muscle and operates continuously throughout a person's life. Both smooth muscle and the heart muscle move by themselves and a person cannot control them. Therefore they are called involuntary muscles.

Holding together

Bone, cartilage, and muscle may be key parts of the human body, but it is the tendons and ligaments that connect these parts and help them to move easily. Tendons connect muscles to bones and ligaments connect bones to each other. Both are strong, flexible bands that are located at the joints.

White and red fibers

Skeletal muscles contain two different types of fiber: white fibers and red fibers. White fibers do not have a good blood supply. They use up their supply of energy very quickly and waste products build up, so they soon become tired. White fibers can contract very quickly for short periods, so they are important for short, fast activities such as sprinting. Red fibers have a good blood supply, so they do not become tired quickly. Red fibers contract more slowly but can keep going for a long time, so they are important for activities that last longer, such as marathon running.

cranial
muscle

◀ **Flex those muscles!**
The muscles in the human body allow all body movements, from the big movements that allow a person to kick a ball to tiny movements such as blinking. As well as moving the bones, muscles also help a person to keep his or her balance and stay upright.

muscles that
move the arm

tendon

muscles
that move
the leg

Key facts:

• The human body contains about 650 muscles, accounting for almost half of the body's weight. When muscles contract they can become just one-third of their actual size.

• Skeletal muscles are not only attached to bone. The face has more than thirty muscles, attached to skin as well as bone. They contract to allow a person to pull his or her face into any expression.

• In some parts of the body, muscles are arranged in rings. These control the size of openings. Rings of muscle control the shapes of the lips and the iris of the eye. They also control openings from the bladder and digestive system so that a person can control when he or she gets rid of body waste.

Moving the body

Skeletal muscle is made up from long, thin strands called fibers. These are bound into bundles, which are held together by an outer layer. Blood vessels run in between the bundles of fibers, bringing oxygen and nutrients that the muscle needs, and carrying away waste chemicals made by the muscle. Nerves are also attached to muscle fibers. These carry messages between the brain and the muscle. To move part of the body, the brain sends a signal to a skeletal muscle telling it to contract. To do this, tiny threads inside the muscle fibers slide past each other, making the whole muscle shorter and fatter.

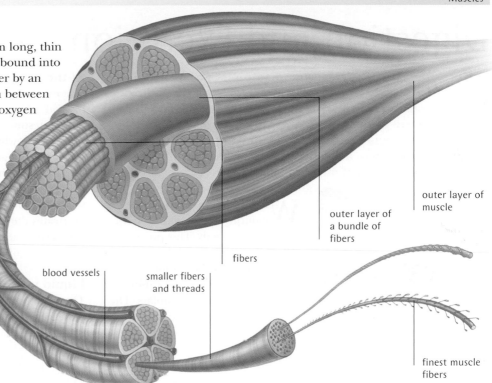

outer layer of muscle

outer layer of a bundle of fibers

fibers

blood vessels

smaller fibers and threads

finest muscle fibers

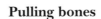

Pulling bones

Bones are moved by muscles. When a person decides to move a bone, one or more muscles attached to it contract. This pulls the bone into a new position. Muscles can only pull bones, they cannot push them. To move a bone back again, it has to be pulled by another muscle. For this reason, muscles work in pairs, with each muscle in the pair having an opposite effect to the other. To raise the lower arm, the biceps muscle at the front of the upper arm contracts, pulling the bone upward. This stretches the triceps muscle at the back of the upper arm. To lower the arm again, the triceps muscles contracts, pulling the bone downward. This stretches the biceps muscle. Many of our movements are more complicated than this and involve more pairs of muscles moving several bones in more than one direction.

biceps contracts, triceps relaxes: lower arm is raised

triceps contracts, biceps relaxes: lower arm is straightened

▲ **Opposing forces**
A pair of muscles work in opposite ways to raise and lower a person's arm.

▲ **Inside muscles**
Muscles are made up of bundles of long, thin fibers. Blood vessels and nerves run between the bundles. The blood vessels bring nutrients and oxygen. The nerves carry messages between the brain and the muscles.

Try these too:

External Body Parts (p 8–9), Bones and Joints (p 10–11), Digestion and Excretion (p 14–15), The Heart and Circulation (p 18–19)

Digestion and Excretion

The body gets rid of waste matter in different ways. The skin gets rid of excess water and salt, we breathe out carbon dioxide and water vapor, the urinary system sends out urine, and the digestive system gets rid of solid waste. The digestive system is responsible for nourishing all parts of the body. It breaks down the food that is eaten, helps the body to absorb the nutrients in the food, and gets rid of any waste matter that remains.

▲ **Four tastes**
Although there are many different flavors in food, there are only four main tastes—sweet, salty, bitter, and sour. Mixing these four tastes together in different ways creates the full range of different flavors that people enjoy in their food.

When we put food into our mouth, we trigger a series of actions in our body. This process is called digestion. An adult usually has 32 teeth in his or her mouth. They are the incisors, the canines, the molars, and the premolars. The incisors and canines help bite and tear the food into small pieces, and the premolars and molars grind the food. The mouth produces saliva, which helps us to break the food down and move it around in the mouth. The saliva turns the food into a mush, making it easy to swallow it.

Down the tube

The food travels down the esophagus, or food pipe, to the stomach, which produces chemicals called enzymes. These enzymes further break down the food. The partly digested food goes from the stomach to the small intestine. Here, it is broken down completely and all the nutrients and water pass through the intestines into the bloodstream. The blood takes these nutrients to other parts of the body. The small intestine uses bile, sent from the gall bladder, and enzymes and acids from the pancreas, to break down the food. Excess fat is converted into fat molecules (by the liver) and fat cells under the skin, and stored for future use.

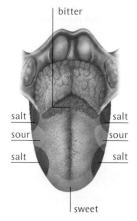

▲ **Taste zones**
Certain areas of the tongue are sensitive to particular flavors.

bitter

salt — salt
sour — sour
salt — salt

sweet

At the very end

The excess water and undigested parts of food, which is termed fiber, are sent to the large intestine. Here, all the remaining water is absorbed, while bacteria present in the intestine change the rest of the waste food into feces. As the excess water is absorbed it causes the feces to harden. The large intestine secretes a slimy substance called mucus that lubricates the feces so that it passes out easily. The feces is sent into the rectum where it is pushed out of the body through the anus.

Liquid waste

The urinary system consists of a pair of kidneys, a bladder, two thin tubes called ureters (which connect the kidneys to the bladder) and a tube called the urethra (which passes the urine out of the body). The kidneys remove the waste matter in blood by filtering it. The waste that it collects is called urine. Urine is a watery substance that contains urea. Too much urea can be harmful to the body. The ureters carry the urine into the urinary bladder. As more and more urine is sent to the bladder, it stretches until it can hold no more. At this point the nerves in the bladder alert the brain that the bladder has to be emptied. A muscle called the sphincter controls the opening between the bladder and the urethra. When the brain receives the message it in turn tells the sphincter to relax and let urine pass through. The bladder squeezes to force the urine down the urethra.

crown

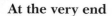

gum
root
bone
capillary
nerve

◀ **Toothy tales**
A human tooth consists of two main parts—crown and root. The crown is the exposed part of the tooth jutting above the gum. It has an outer covering of enamel, which is the hardest substance in the human body. Inside the tooth there is a cavity filled with tissue, blood vessels and nerve fibers. This region is called the pulp and is very sensitive.

▶ Long and winding
The small intestine is the longest section of the digestive tract. The total length of the tract is 40 feet (12 meters). The small intestine alone constitutes about 16 feet (5 meters) of it.

Oral cavity

Tongue

Pharynx

Pancreas

The pancreas is a small but very important organ situated behind the stomach. It releases enzymes that break up proteins, fats, and carbohydrates into the small intestine. In fact, if the pancreas does not produce these enzymes, a person can starve even if they are overeating! The pancreas also produces insulin and glucagons, which maintain the glucose level in the body and prevent diabetes. Pancreatic juices also contain sodium bicarbonate, a chemical that can neutralize acid in the stomach.

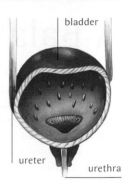

bladder

ureter

urethra

▲ Storing urine
The bladder can store about 3 pints (1.5 liters) of urine, or even more.

esophagus

liver

stomach

gall bladder

duodenum

pancreas

large intestine

colon

small intestine

rectum

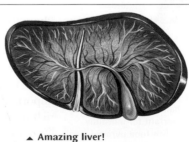

▲ Amazing liver!
The liver is the largest internal organ, and probably one of the busiest. It processes sugar and fats for storage, manufactures bile for digestion, and contains a reservoir of blood that is released if the body loses too much.

Key facts:

• The digestive system is made up of a long tube that starts at the mouth and ends at the anus. This tube, called the alimentary canal, is about 40 feet (12 meters) long—that is five times the height of an average adult.

• Each bean-shaped kidney contains about one million filters, or nephrons. Both kidneys work continually to clean blood. About 42 gallons (190 liters) of blood pass through the kidneys every day.

• On the right side of the lower abdomen, attached to the large intestine, is a short tube called the appendix. The appendix plays no known part in the digestion process, or any of the other functions of the body.

Try these too:

External Body Parts (p 8–9), Bones and Joints (p 10–11), A Balanced Diet (p 16–17), Falling Sick (p 28–29)

A Balanced Diet

Diet is everything a person eats and drinks. It should provide the body with all the nutrients needed for being active, growing and staying healthy. Different types of food provide different nutrients, but no food provides everything. It makes sense to eat a range of foods to provide the body with a mixture of nutrients. A diet that contains all the nutrients a person needs is called a balanced diet.

The food you eat contains a huge range of different chemicals. However, only a few of these, known as nutrients, are needed to keep us healthy. Nutrients come from five kinds of substances found in food: protein, fats, carbohydrates, vitamins, and minerals.

Proteins

Proteins are found in foods such as meats, fish, eggs, and nuts. Foods made from milk are also good sources of protein. Proteins are the building blocks for the body. They help a person to grow strong and to repair damage such as cut skin and broken bones. It is a good idea to try to eat at least two portions of protein-rich food every day.

▲ Essential for health
The body only needs tiny amounts of vitamins and minerals, but they are essential for health. They are found in many different foods, but fruits and vegetables are some of the best sources.

▶ Eating healthy
A balanced diet is very important for a healthy life. This food pyramid explains the kind and amount of nutrients required each day to keep a person healthy.

▶ Amino acids
Proteins are made from simpler chemicals called amino acids, strung together rather like beads on a necklace. When proteins are digested, the amino acids are separated. The body can then rearrange the amino acids in different orders to make all the different proteins that it needs.

Vitamins and Minerals

There are fifteen main vitamins, each of which is needed to maintain a healthy body. The most important vitamins are A (needed for healthy eyes and skin), B (for healthy skin and general good health), C (healing cuts and strengthening the body's defenses), and D (for strong teeth and bones).

Minerals are another group of chemicals that the body needs to stay healthy. There are about twenty minerals that are essential to the body. One of the most important is iron. Foods that are rich in iron include meat, eggs, liver, and leafy green vegetables. The body needs iron to make a protein called hemoglobin. This forms part of the blood that carries oxygen around the body.

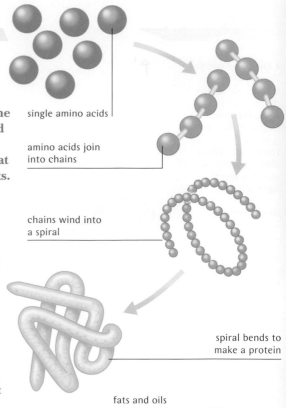

single amino acids

amino acids join into chains

chains wind into a spiral

spiral bends to make a protein

fats and oils

sugars

milk and milk products, meat, fish

fruit and vegetables

▲ **Water of life**
The toxins that enter the body are dissolved in water and flushed out of the body through the excretory system. Therefore, it is important that a person drinks at least eight glasses of water every day.

Carbohydrates

Starches and sugars belong to a group of chemicals called carbohydrates. They provide energy and are found in a lot of foods. Foods that contain starch are good at making a person feel full. Starchy foods include bread, pasta, rice, and cereals. Many doctors think that starchy foods should make up about two-fifths of our diet.

Sugars make foods taste sweet, and are found in foods such as cakes, biscuits, sweets, and fizzy drinks. It is important not to eat too many sugary foods, as they are very bad for the teeth. Also, a small portion of sugary food can provide a lot of energy, so it is easy to eat more than the body needs without realizing it. Sugary foods and drinks can give a quick burst of energy just when it is needed, but they do not satisfy for very long.

grains

▲ **Eat your spuds**
Some vegetables, like potatoes, are also good sources of starch. These foods provide energy, but they are not bad for the teeth. Also, as the body can only digest them slowly, a person feels full for a long time and so it is easy to control how much her or she eats.

Fats and Oils

Fats and oils are found in fried foods, and also in many other foods such as dairy products and nuts. They are an important part of our diet because they provide a lot of energy as well as other important chemicals that our bodies need. Fats also help to keep the body warm. There are two types of fat: saturated and unsaturated. Saturated fats are found in foods that come from animals, including dairy products and fatty meat. Unsaturated fats are found in non-animal foods like nuts and vegetable oils. Many doctors think that unsaturated fats are better for the health than saturated fats.

Key facts:

• Carbohydrates are made up of the chemical elements carbon, hydrogen, and oxygen. In a well-balanced diet, carbohydrates should give a person about half the energy needed.

• Calcium is a mineral essential to health. It is found in dairy products. It is part of the material that bones and teeth are made from. Without calcium, bones become weak and brittle

•The energy in food is measured in units called calories. A calorie is the amount of energy needed to raise one gram of water one celsius degree. If a person takes in more calories than his or her body burns, most of the excess calories will be stored in the body as fat. If a person takes in fewer calories than his or her body burns, the body will burn stored fat for energy.

Try these too:

External Body Parts (p 8–9), Bones and Joints (p 10–11), Digestion and Excretion (p 14–15), Falling Sick (p 28–29)

The Heart and Circulation

The heart is one of the most important organs in the human body. The heart, along with numerous blood vessels, keeps the body healthy and fit. Any breakdown in the heart and circulatory system will result in almost immediate death.

Key facts:

• The heart is only as big as a fist. It begins functioning from the time the fetus is formed and does not stop until the person dies. During this time it beats more than two and half billion times.

• The lungs and the heart need clean blood and nutrients to work well. The heart gets back the clean, oxygenated blood it needs through the coronary arteries, and the lungs get it through the bronchial arteries.

• There are blood cells in every living part of your body. If you took an average adult's blood vessels and laid them all out in a straight line, they would stretch nearly 60 miles (100 kilometers).

• English physician William Harvey (1578–1657) discovered how blood circulates in human beings and other mammals.

The heart is a muscular organ situated toward the left side of the chest, between the lungs. It is responsible for pumping blood to all parts of the body. The blood that goes out of the heart carries oxygen and nutrients, and the blood that comes back is full of carbon dioxide. The human heart is divided into four chambers. A muscle known as the septum divides the heart lengthwise into two chambers. These chambers are in turn divided horizontally by valves that can open and close. The chambers on top are called atria, and those at the bottom are called ventricles. Large blood vessels called arteries carry clean blood from the heart, while veins bring unclean blood back to the heart.

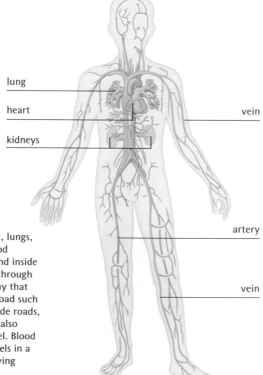

lung
heart
kidneys
vein
artery
vein

▶ **One-way system**
This diagram shows the heart, lungs, and major blood vessels. Blood cannot move randomly around inside the body. Instead, it travels through blood vessels. In the same way that there are different types of road such as motorways, main roads, side roads, and country lanes, there are also different types of blood vessel. Blood flows through the blood vessels in a one–way system, always moving along in the same direction.

The path of circulation

Blood containing carbon dioxide is brought to the heart by the superior and inferior vena cava, or "heart veins." This impure blood enters the right atrium. When the atrium is full, the valve opens and the blood flows down into the right ventricle. From here the blood is sent to the lungs through the pulmonary artery. The lungs breathe out the carbon dioxide that comes with the blood and breathe in the oxygen from the air. The oxygenated blood then re-enters the heart, into the left atrium, through the pulmonary veins. When the atrium is full, the valve connecting it to the left ventricle is opened and the clean blood flows down into it. The blood is then sent out into the body through the aorta, which is the largest artery in the human body. The left ventricle is more muscular than the rest of the heart because it has to pump with greater force to send the clean blood to all parts of the body. The process of receiving unclean blood, getting it cleaned and finally pumping it back into the body is called a cardiac cycle.

Transport network

The circulatory system is a complex network consisting of delicate tubes that carry blood to all parts of the body and back to the heart. This system is made up of the heart, arteries, veins, and capillaries. Arteries and veins, as we know, carry blood to the heart and back.

▼ **The number game**
Organs that are more active than others require more capillaries.

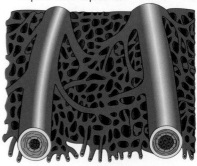

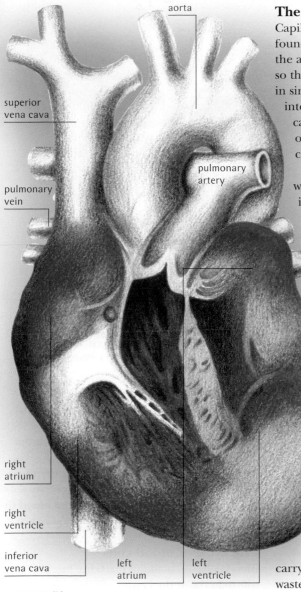

aorta

superior
vena cava

pulmonary
artery

pulmonary
vein

right
atrium

right
ventricle

inferior
vena cava

left
atrium

left
ventricle

▲ Hearty life
As well as pumping blood, the heart also secretes
a hormone called atrial natriuretic factor, or ANF,
which regulates blood pressure.

The tiny carriers

Capillaries are fragile blood vessels that are
found throughout the body—they connect
the arteries and veins. The capillaries are
so thin that blood cells travel through them
in single file. Oxygen in the blood is passed
into the tissues through the thin walls of the
capillaries. Similarly, carbon dioxide and
other chemical wastes also pass into the
capillaries to be taken away.

The blood is taken to the kidneys,
where the urea in it is filtered and made
into urine. The filtered blood then goes
to the small intestine. Here, the nutrients
from digested food enter the blood,
before it goes to the liver. The liver
absorbs the nutrients and converts them
for storage. It also reduces the effect of
harmful substances, like enzymes,
which come from the intestine.
The blood is then sent through
the inferior vena cava back
into the heart.

Supplying the heart

The heart is protected by an
outer layer called the
pericardium, which lubricates it
and holds it firmly in place. Just
like every other muscle in the
body, the heart needs a constant
supply of oxygen and nutrients.
Waste products made by the heart
muscle also have to be removed. The
heart has its own special blood vessels
carrying oxygen to it and carrying away its
waste. These are called the coronary arteries
and veins. They form a network around the
outside of the heart, so that blood can reach
every part of it.

▾ When the heart beats
The contraction of the
muscles of the left and
right atria forces blood
into the ventricles. The
pressure in the ventricles
increase, forcing the
valves between the atria
and ventricles to close. At
the same time, the aortic
and pulmonary valves are
forced open to carry the
blood out. This opening
and closing of valves
causes the characteristic
lub-dub sound made by
the heart as it beats.

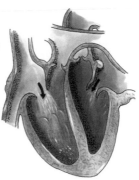

Blood flowing
into the ventricles

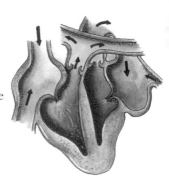

Blood flowing
out of the ventricles

Heart attacks

A heart attack is most often caused by a
blockage in the coronary blood vessels,
preventing blood from reaching part of the
heart muscle. Without fresh blood, this part
of the heart dies. This affects the whole
heart and stops it from beating properly.

The first sign of a heart attack is often a
severe chest pain. The patient's left hand
and arm often tingle too, and they may find
it hard to breathe. The sooner the patient
receives treatment, the better their chances
of making a full recovery.

Try these too:

Muscles (p 12–13), Blood
(p 20–21), The Lungs
and Respiration
(p 22–23), The Brain
and Nervous System
(p 24–25)

Blood

Blood is the human body's internal transport system and it defends the body against germs. It helps to control the amounts of water and chemicals in the body, and also helps to control the body's temperature. A single drop of blood contains millions and millions of tiny cells called "formed elements" in a clear, watery liquid. There are three formed elements: red blood cells, white blood cells, and platelets.

[handwritten annotations: "lives for 3 months", "destroyed by spleen & liver", "Life Varies some day n two some 2-3 months very few 7 a year"]

red blood cells

white blood cells

platelet

▲ **Oxygen carriers**
Red blood cells, also called erythrocytes, make up nearly half of the volume of a person's blood. Red blood cells collect oxygen from the lungs and release it to cells in the body.

Key facts:

• Red blood cells are extremely small. Each one is only about 0.0003 inches (0.0075 millimeters) across, making red blood cells among the smallest cells in the body.

• The body contains many billions of white blood cells. Normally the blood has only about one white blood cell for every 800 red blood cells, but when the body is fighting infection, the number of white blood cells increases.

• Hemophilia is a disease that prevents blood from clotting. A hemophiliac's blood does not clot properly because one of the clotting factors is missing from his or her blood. It is a hereditary disease. Women can pass hemophilia to their children, but usually only males suffer from it.

The clear, watery liquid that all the formed elements float around in is called plasma. It contains many different chemicals and nutrients, which it carries to every part of the body. Waste chemicals are also carried in the plasma until they are removed by the liver or kidneys.

Formed elements

Red blood cells are like discs that have been squashed at the top and bottom. They are tiny—125 side by side would be needed to make a line 0.04 inch (1 millimeter) long! Red blood cells carry oxygen around the body. It is their color that makes the blood look red. White blood cells can be many different shapes and sizes. They are the

◄ **Blood ingredients**
These are the three formed elements of the blood.

body's defense system. Some release special chemicals to destroy germs like bacteria and viruses. Some surround any particles that should not be in the body, and destroy them. Some develop a chemical "memory" of germs so that they can attack them quickly the next time they find them. Platelets are very, very tiny fragments of cells. They help the blood to clot and form a scab.

Life cycle of blood cells

Blood cells are made in the bone marrow, the soft material at the center of some bones. Some travel to other parts of the body to finish developing. Some white blood cells only live for a day or two. Others may live for two or three months, while a very few may live for over a year. Red blood cells live for about three months. At the end of their life, blood cells are destroyed by the spleen and liver. Some of the chemicals they were made from are stored or reused, while others leave the body in the urine.

Platelets and clotting

When a person receives a cut, blood oozes out of the cut skin. Unless the cut is very deep, the blood soon stops flowing. It becomes sticky and eventually a scab forms over the surface of the cut. The platelets in the blood contain special chemicals called clotting factors to make the blood stick together, or clot. They also make a mesh to cover the cut and form a scab. Below this, the cut heals as new skin is made. When the cut is completely healed, the scab falls off. If a scab is picked at, it may damage the new skin that is forming beneath it.

Blood groups

Although human beings have the same kind of blood, there are some differences that can only be seen with the help of a microscope. Based on these differences, blood has been divided into four groups—A, B, AB, and O. In addition, some people have a certain blood protein present in their blood. This is called the Rhesus, or Rh, factor. Blood types that have this blood protein or the Rh factor have a "+" sign and those that do not have a "-" sign, for example A+ or A-, O+, or O-, and so on. If blood from different groups is mixed together, they can react against each other. This would make a person very ill.

Giving blood

A constant supply of blood is needed for blood transfusions. To give blood, people go to a blood donation center. The donor sits or lies down and a sterile needle is put into a vein at the inside of the elbow. A collecting bag is attached to the other end of the needle via a plastic tube. Blood flows out of the vein, down the tube, and into the bag. Blood is stored at "blood banks." Donated blood may be refrigerated and stored as whole blood or separated into its constituent parts.

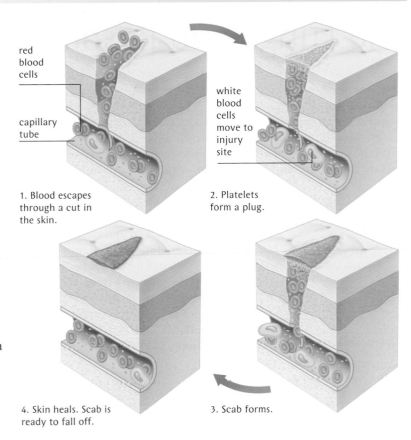

1. Blood escapes through a cut in the skin.
2. Platelets form a plug.
4. Skin heals. Scab is ready to fall off.
3. Scab forms.

▲ **Scab formation**
This diagram shows how platelets help a scab form over a cut.

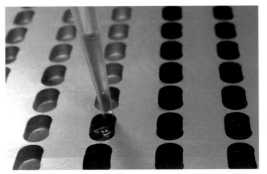

◄ **Blood typing**
Chemical tests are carried out to establish the blood group of a sample of donated blood.

Blood transfusions

It can be dangerous to lose a lot of blood, either through an accident or because of an operation. Doctors may use blood from a blood donor to replace the lost blood. This transfer of blood from one person to another is called a blood transfusion. It is important that the blood groups of patient and donor are matched so that the patient does not receive blood that their own blood will react against.

Try these too:

External Body Parts (p 8–9), Bones and Joints (p 10–11), Digestion and Excretion (p 14–15), The Heart and Circulation (p 18–19)

The Lungs and Respiration

Humans need to keep breathing all the time. Breathing in provides our bodies with an essential gas called oxygen. Breathing out allows us to get rid of a waste gas called carbon dioxide. Breathing also allows us to talk, sing, and make other noises. Breathing, also called respiration, is carried out by parts of the body that together make up the respiratory system. They include the mouth and nose, throat, windpipe, and lungs.

Key facts:

• An average person takes about 900 breaths every hour of his or her life. Over a lifetime of 70 years, that works out at over 550 million breaths.

•At rest, about 30 cubic inches (0.5 liter) of air passes in and out of the lungs with each breath. If an adult breathes in as much air as possible, then breathes out as much as possible, he or she will breathe out about 287 cubic inches (4.7 liters) of air.

•Even when a person breathes out as much air as he or she can, the elastic tissue in the lungs is still slightly stretched and some air remains in the lungs. This remaining air stops the lungs from collapsing and becoming unable to take air in.

The nose is the main route for air to enter and leave the body. When breathing in, air is sucked into the nostrils. Once air has entered the nose, it moves down into the throat. The top part of the throat is called the pharynx. This is a hollow tube with strong muscular walls and a moist lining of mucus. Air travels from the nose and mouth, through the pharynx, to the trachea (windpipe). At the top of the trachea is the larynx.

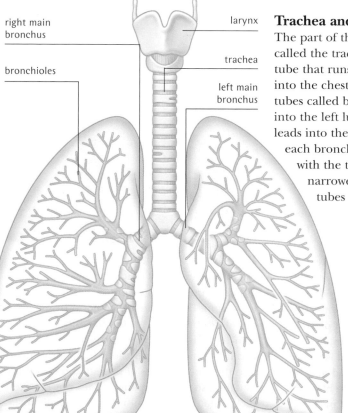

right main bronchus

bronchioles

larynx

trachea

left main bronchus

▶ **Branching bronchi**
This diagram shows the trachea, bronchi, and lungs. Both the trachea and the bronchi have muscle and fiber walls and C-shaped rings of cartilage for support.

nose

mouth

bronchi

trachea

left lung

right lung

heart

ribs

diaphragm

▲ **Not only for oxygen**
This diagram shows how the lungs and airways are positioned inside the chest. Breathing is important for other reasons other than getting oxygen. It enables people to talk, sing, laugh, and whistle.

Trachea and bronchi

The part of the windpipe below the larynx is called the trachea. The trachea is a hollow tube that runs from the bottom of the throat into the chest. It branches into two narrower tubes called bronchi. The left bronchus leads into the left lung and the right bronchus leads into the right lung. Inside the lungs, each bronchus branches again and again, with the tubes getting narrower and narrower at each stage. The tiniest tubes are called bronchioles.

▲ **Breath control**
Playing a wind instrument such as this one requires careful control of expiration (breathing out).

The voicebox

Another name for the larynx is the voice-box. It is made up of a framework of stiff cartilage. The vocal cords are attached to this framework. When a person breathes, air flows between the vocal cords. They are apart, so the air flows freely and there is no noise. When a person wants to speak, neck muscles move the cartilage frame, pulling the vocal cords tighter and closer together. As air flows through them, it makes the vocal cords vibrate, which makes a noise. The tighter the vocal cords are pulled, the higher the sounds they make.

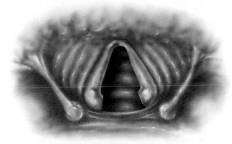

vocal cords apart—no sound made

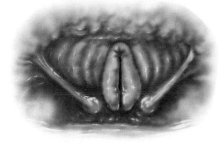

vocal cords closed—sounds made

Lungs

The lungs are two spongelike organs that take up most of the space inside the chest. The left and right lungs are linked by the bronchi. Air enters and leaves each lung via the bronchi and bronchioles. The very narrowest bronchioles branch again to form even tinier tubes. At the end of each are round, hollow spaces called alveoli. These are clustered together at the end of the bronchiole. Each alveolus is surrounded by a network of very thin blood vessels called capillaries.

Gas Exchange

The body needs a continuous supply of oxygen. It also needs to get rid of a waste gas called carbon dioxide. This gas exchange happens inside the lungs. Oxygen and carbon dioxide travel around the body in the blood. The pulmonary artery brings deoxygenated blood to the lungs from the heart. The deoxygenated blood travels through smaller and smaller blood vessels and at last reaches the capillaries around the alveoli. Blood capillaries are wrapped very closely around the alveoli. Both the blood vessels and the alveoli have very thin walls that gases can easily pass through. When a person breathes in, the alveoli fill up with air. Oxygen moves from the space inside the alveoli, through the alveolar wall, through the blood capillary wall and into the blood. It gets picked up and carried away by red blood cells. At the same time, carbon dioxide in the blood does the exact opposite. It passes out of the blood and into the space inside the alveoli.

The carbon dioxide leaves the body when a person breathes out. The oxygenated blood is carried to the heart in the pulmonary vein. The heart then pumps it around the rest of the body, so that every organ and muscle receives a continuous supply of fresh oxygen. Organs and muscles constantly produce carbon dioxide, which is collected by the blood. This deoxygenated blood travels back to the heart and then to the lungs, where it loses carbon dioxide and collects oxygen. And so the cycle continues.

capillary carrying deoxygenated blood

alveolus

carbon dioxide

capillary carrying oxygenated blood

oxygen

▲ **Exchanging gases**
This diagram shows how gas exchange happens inside the alveoli. Although each blood capillary is very narrow, there are billions of them, so the amount of blood passing through the lungs at any one time is very large.

▼ **Asthma**
Many people suffer from asthma, a breathing disorder caused by an allergy to airborne particles such as pollen. In an asthma attack, the airways get inflamed, making it harder to breathe. An inhaler can help control asthma.

Try these too:

Bones and Joints (p 10–11), Digestion and Excretion (p 14–15), The Heart and Circulation (p 18–19), Falling Sick (p 28–29)

The Brain and Nervous System

The nervous system is the messaging system of the body. The brain and spinal cord are the most important part of this system and are together called the central nervous system. They are supported by millions of nerves and the sense organs—ears, eyes, nose, tongue and skin.

▼ It's just cerebral
The cerebrum is the largest and most important part of the human brain. The front part of the cerebrum, known as frontal lobe, is responsible for speech, thought, and emotion. The parietal lobe, located behind the frontal lobe, helps to understand touch and feel pain.

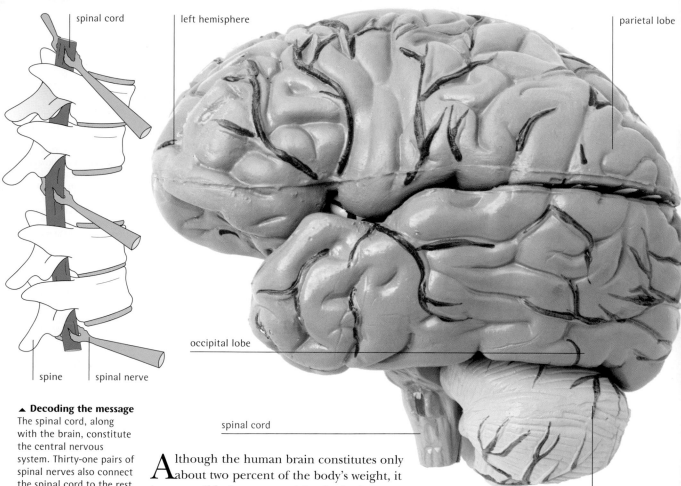

spinal cord

left hemisphere

parietal lobe

occipital lobe

spinal cord

spine

spinal nerve

cerebellum

▲ Decoding the message
The spinal cord, along with the brain, constitute the central nervous system. Thirty-one pairs of spinal nerves also connect the spinal cord to the rest of the body. These nerves help to carry messages to and from the spinal cord to other parts of the body. In most cases, the spinal cord conveys the impulses to the brain for processing. However, in reflex actions, such as pulling one's hand away from fire, the spinal cord processes the impulses.

Although the human brain constitutes only about two percent of the body's weight, it is responsible for every activity the body undertakes. It plays a role in every thought that humans think, every memory that they have, and every skill that they develop. The brain also determines a person's personality. In short, a human being cannot function without a brain. This essential organ is also the most vulnerable and delicate part of the body. Even the smallest injury can affect brain's function.

Therefore, the brain is well protected. Three membranes called meninges surround the brain. The space between the meninges and the brain is filled with cerebrospinal fluid, which absorbs shock and protects the brain from infections. The skull forms the outermost layer of protection.

▶ Nerve fibers
A neuron consists of a cell body with a nucleus and one or more fibers. These fibers vary greatly in length. The fibers that carry impulses toward the nucleus are called dendrites, while those which carry impulses away from the nucleus are known as axons.

dendrite

axon

nucleus

cell body

Dissecting the brain

The brain consists of three main parts—cerebrum, cerebellum, and brain stem. The grey outer part of the cerebrum is called the cortex. This is where information from other parts of the body is received. Within the cortex is a large white matter, which sends messages to the other parts of the body. The cerebrum is further sub-divided into several sections, and each section is responsible for a particular function—each communicates with a particular sense organ. Below the cerebrum, toward the back, is the cerebellum. This part of the brain controls our body movements. The brain is connected to the spinal cord through the brain stem. All involuntary activities like breathing, heartbeat, and digestion are controlled by the brain stem. It also takes messages from the brain to the spinal cord, which runs from the brain to the lower back, through the backbone. The spinal cord has an outer white layer and an inner grey layer, within which is cerebrospinal fluid. The spinal cord carries information to the brain and messages from the brain to the other organs.

Nerves carry information from all parts of the body to the spinal cord and the brain, and messages back to the organs. They are made up of several million cells, called neurons. Nerves form the body's peripheral nervous system.

How we learn and remember

When you read something, signals are sent from your eyes to your brain. Nerve cells in the brain are activated and the brain makes sense of what you see. If you read the words again and again, the same nerve cells are repeatedly activated and connections between them are made. A similar process happens when you repeat an action many times. This allows us to learn things and remember them. The more we repeat something, the stronger and more firmly established the connections within the brain become. For example, a toddler does not know precisely which muscles to move and how to co-ordinate the movements in order to pick up a pencil and make a mark. By experimenting and trying again and again, he or she gradually finds this out. With practice, the child's drawing and writing skills improve.

Hormones

The endocrine glands play a very important role in the nervous system. These glands release chemicals called hormones, which travel to the brain and other parts of the body. These hormones affect our bodily functions. There are eight major glands in the human body that produce hormones. Some glands are present only in men and others can be found only in women. The hormones affect the growth of bones and muscles, the balance of minerals and chemicals in the body, and reproduction.

Key facts:

• The right side of the brain is used more by people who are creative, whereas people who are good at mathematics and science tend to use the left side of their brain more often.

• Messages are passed in the form of electrical signals through neurons. However, while moving from one neuron to the next, the electrical signal has to change into a chemical signal. This is because neurons do not touch each other.

• Endocrine glands are ductless glands. This means that they do not have tubes to transport the hormones. Hormones travel through the body by entering the blood stream.

▲ As a person repeats particular movements, such as playing a chord on a guitar, connections between nerve cells in the brain become more established. This process involves the cerebellum, which is linked by nerves to the diencephalon, the spinal cord, and the body muscles.

Try these too:

External Body Parts (p 8–9),
Muscles (p 12–13),
Sensing the World (p 26–27)

Sensing the World

Humans have five senses: sight, hearing, touch, taste, and smell. These enable us to find out about the world around us. Each sense relies on a sense organ to collect information and send it to the brain. Our eyes collect light information and our ears collect sound information. Receptors in our skin collect information about temperature, texture, and pressure. Our tongues and noses collect information about chemicals in our food and drink and in the air around us.

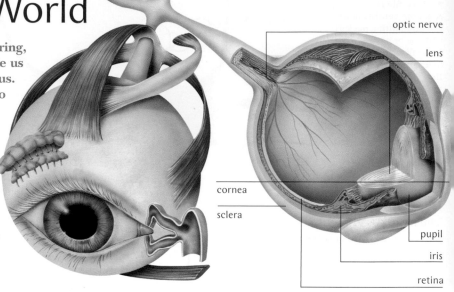

optic nerve

lens

cornea

sclera

pupil

iris

retina

Key facts:

• The earlobes have few pain receptors. Pressure can be felt on the lobes if they are squeezed between the fingers, but if one presses on only a small area, no pain can be felt.

• The eye's retina has two types of receptor cell: rods and cones. The 120 million rods help us to make out shapes. The 6 million cones enable us to see colors. Cones work only in bright light, which is why it is hard to see colors in dim light but it is still possible to make out shapes.

• The inner ear has a complex system of fluid-filled canals ending in a spiral called the cochlea. Vibrations from the ear bones move hair cells in the cochlea. These movements are converted to electric impulses which the brain then interprets to work out the direction of the sound.

When a sense organ is stimulated by its own type of information, it responds by sending out an electrical signal. This travels along a nerve to the appropriate sensory area of the brain. The sensory area and association area then work together to make sense of the information and interpret it.

Sight

When light enters the eye, an image is formed on the inside layer, or retina, of the eye. The retina contains receptor cells that are sensitive to light and these respond by sending signals along the optic nerve to the sight sensory area in the brain. The sight sensory and association areas work together to interpret the information and work out what a person is seeing. Because the two eyes each get a slightly different view, the brain can work out a three-dimensional view of things.

▶ **The art of listening**
Hearing enables us to enjoy music, use language, and hear sounds that alert us to danger. All sounds travel as vibrations in the air. Receptors in the ear pick up these vibrations and send signals to the brain, which interprets the signals as sounds.

▲ **Eye structure**
The eye is made up of a colored iris, the sclera, and the cornea, which is a clear, protective layer. The black part in the middle of the iris is a hole called the pupil. Behind the pupil is the lens, which focuses light rays onto the retina at the back of the eyeball.

Hearing

When sounds reach the ear, they make parts inside the ear vibrate. The ear converts these vibrations to signals, which are sent along the auditory nerve to the hearing sensory area in the brain. The hearing sensory and association areas work together to interpret the signals and work out what a person is hearing. Because the ears are on opposite sides of the head, the brain can pinpoint exactly what place the sound came from.

Touch

Nerve endings in the skin respond to light touch, pressure, heat, cold, vibration, and chemicals. There are several different types of nerve endings, each of which only responds to one type of stimulus. When a nerve ending detects its own special stimulus it responds by sending a signal to the touch sensory area of the brain. The brain then works out what a person has felt and where he or she felt it.

▲ **Soft touch**
Nerve endings in the skin detect the silky softness of the cat's fur and send a signal to the brain.

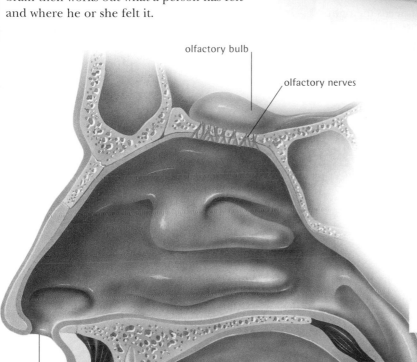

olfactory bulb

olfactory nerves

nostril

Sight problems

People who have defective cones in their retinas are said to be color blind. They may be able to see some colors and not others. Very few such people are not able to see any colors at all. Other sight problems, such as farsightedness and nearsightedness, occur when the lens does not focus light on the retina properly. With farsightedness, the lens needs to thicken to focus on things that are near. With nearsightedness, the lens needs to become thinner to focus on things that are far away. The lens's ability to thicken and thin can decline with age, even in people who have good vision when young.

◀ Molecules from the substance being smelt enter the nose through the nostrils and hit the endings of the olfactory nerves. These carry information to the olfactory bulb, which passes them to the cerebrum for processing.

Taste and Smell

Taste buds in the surface of the tongue detect chemicals in food and drink. Receptors in the lining of the nose detect chemicals in the air. When a person eats or drinks, and when air wafts past the nose, signals are sent to the brain. The brain then works out what the person has tasted or smelt. The ability to taste food is the result of a complicated mixture of signals from both tongue and nose.

◀ Humans can detect about 10,000 different smells.

Try these too:

External Body Parts (p 8–9), Bones and Joints (p 10–11), Digestion and Excretion (p 14–15), The Brain and Nervous System (p 24–25)

27

Falling Sick

When all our organs, systems, bones, and muscles are working well, we enjoy good health. However, when any one of these has trouble, it affects other parts of the body as well— and we suffer from discomfort or disease.

Key facts:

• In 1796, Edward Jenner, an English doctor, invented the vaccine to fight smallpox. He noticed that people who had had cowpox, a mild disease, did not get smallpox. So he inoculated a small boy with the cowpox virus and, after a few days, he inoculated him with smallpox only to prove his theory correct. Vaccines have put an end to smallpox, one of the most infectious diseases known to man. They have also reduced the occurrence of polio, measles, mumps, rubella and chickenpox.

• When we suffer from pain, the hypothalamus and the pituitary glands of the endocrine system produce chemicals called endorphins. Endorphins are natural painkillers that act on the nervous system and lessen pain.

• Doctors sometimes give tablets called placebos to treat illnesses. Placebos do not contain any medication. They are just used to reassure the patient and make them believe that they will recover.

The human body is much like any other machine. It needs the right fuel at the right time. It also needs to be exercised regularly and looked after well. We can fall ill for many reasons. Bad eating habits, no exercise, and lack of hygiene can cause several of the illnesses that we suffer from. An unbalanced or unhealthy diet slows down the working of our organs and results in diseases like diabetes and hypertension. Similarly, lack of exercise makes our bodies stiff and inflexible, and more prone to diseases like osteoporosis and spondylitis.

Alien attacks

Not all diseases are caused by carelessness alone. Sometimes diseases are caused by harmful viruses or bacteria entering our circulatory system. These may enter our bodies from others who are unwell, from food that has not been cooked or stored properly, or from our surroundings. Infectious diseases include the common cold, pneumonia, and flu, as well as more life-threatening illnesses such as cholera, typhoid, tuberculosis, and AIDS.

Body breakdown

Another cause of disease is body malfunction. Sometimes organs speed up their functions, slow down, or stop working. This causes imbalances in the body because of too much or too little of certain chemicals, leading to depression and thyroidism. Cancer occurs when bad cells in a specific part of the body multiply swiftly and destroy the good cells.

▲ **Keeping fit**
Exercising helps you to stay fit. Routine exercise strengthens the muscles and improves the functioning of the other organs in the body.

▲ **Stay protected**
Some sporting activities can involve risks. Wearing the right protective clothing can help to reduce these risks and prevent serious accidents and injuries.

Diagnosing disease

As the number of diseases keeps increasing, science finds more and more ways to understand and treat the human body. Early doctors treated patients after checking their pulse and the color of their eyes and tongue. Today, doctors diagnose diseases using complex and more precise equipment like ultrasonographs, CT scanners, and endoscopes. The endoscope, a slim instrument with a camera, is inserted into the body so that doctors can have a close look at the organs inside.

▼ Checking up
People usually visit doctors when they are not keeping well. They can also go for routine check-ups to make sure that their body is functioning properly.

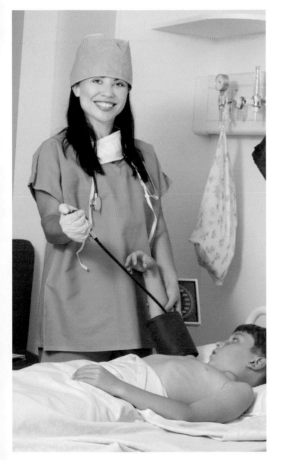

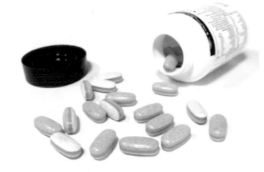

▲ Bitter pill
Swallowing that pill can be very hard. Pills usually leave a bitter taste in the mouth. Some, however, have a smooth gelatinous covering that contains the bitter medicine inside. These capsules are also easy to swallow. Once the pill enters the body, the gelatin case is dissolved by the digestive juices to release the medicine

Fighting back

When infections and disease attack the body, its first response is to fight back. In the process, the body raises its own temperature to kill the infectious bodies that have entered the bloodstream. The white blood cells immediately start attacking the alien bodies in an attempt to kill the infection. These cells even make special antibodies, or proteins, that can match the strength of the infections and fight against them. However, the immune system is not always able to fight the illness all by itself. Therefore, we have to help it by taking medicines. Medicines can be in the form of pills or syrup. They mostly contain chemicals that help to fight diseases. Some medicines can be bought from supermarkets, while the stronger ones can be bought only at a pharmacy, and with a doctor's prescription.

Being prepared

Some illnesses can be avoided by taking medication beforehand. This can be in the form of a vaccination. Vaccinations are injections containing a strain of weak bacteria that causes a particular disease. The injected bacteria immunizes the body and prevents similar bacteria from attacking it. Diseases like measles, mumps, hepatitis, and tetanus can be avoided by vaccination.

▲ ▼ Sting of health
Apart from introducing disease-fighting agents through oral medications like syrups and pills, doctors can also inject them into the body using syringes. Liquid medicine is administered through a hollow needle into the skin, muscles, or directly into the bloodstream through the veins.

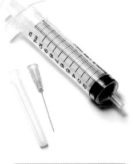

Try these too:

External Body Parts (p 8–9), Bones and Joints (p 10–11), Muscles (p 12–13), Digestion and Excretion (p 14–15) A Balanced Diet (p 16–17), The Heart and Circulation (p 18–19), The Brain and Nervous System (p 24–25)

Index